Tad's Dot to Dot Pad

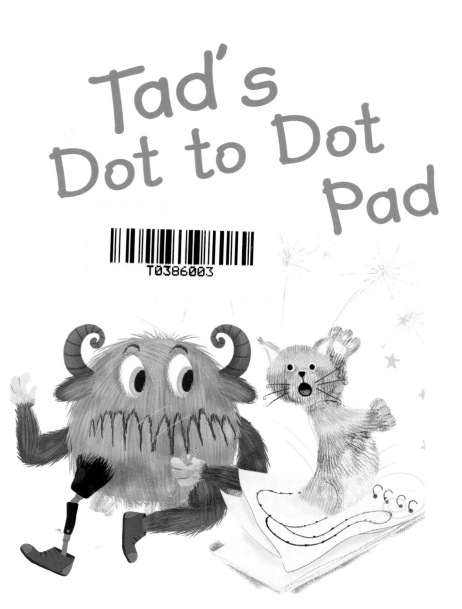

Written by Catherine Baker

Illustrated by Mel Armstrong

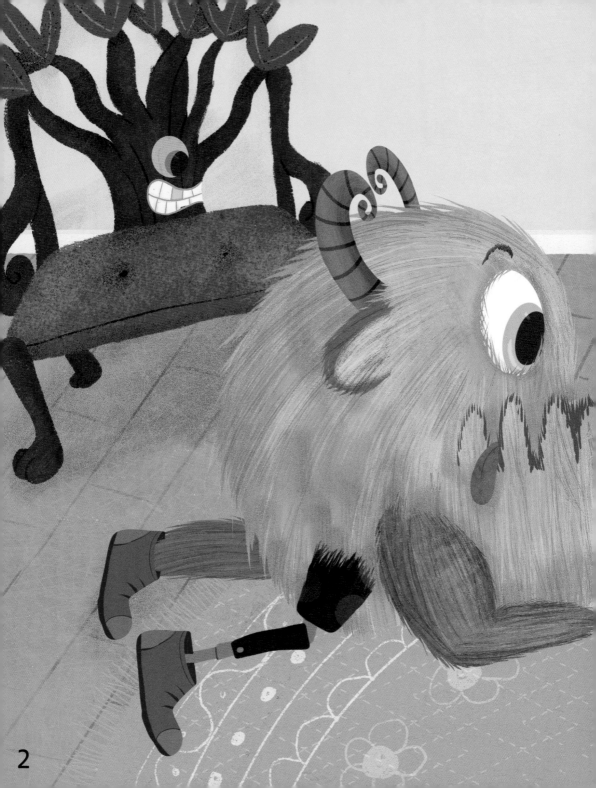

2

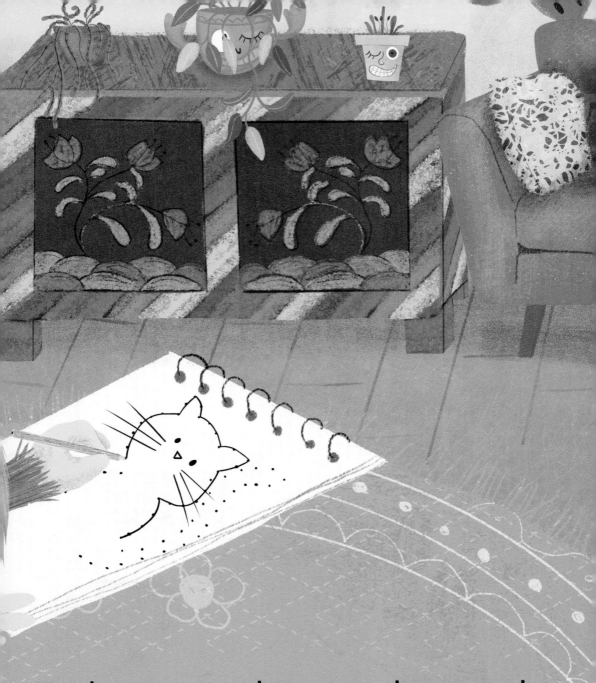

Tad got a dot to dot pad.

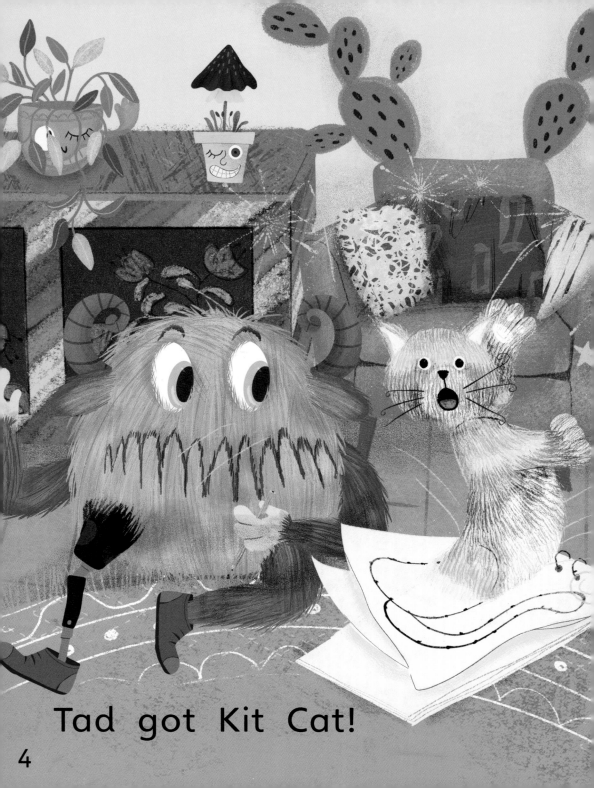

Tad got Kit Cat!

4

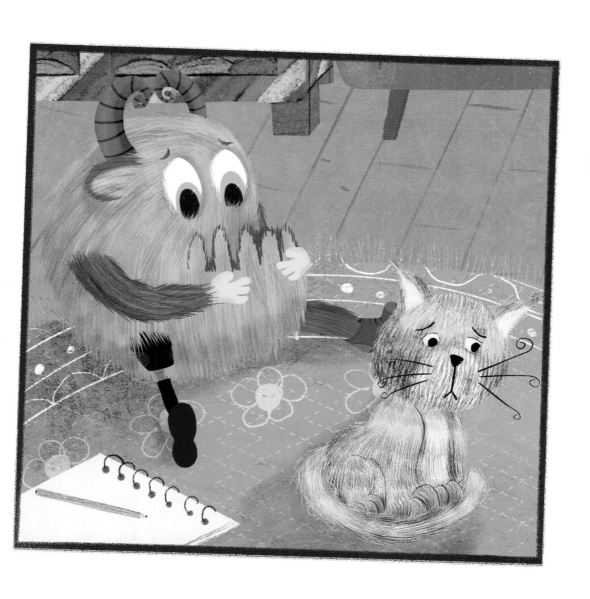

Kit is sad!

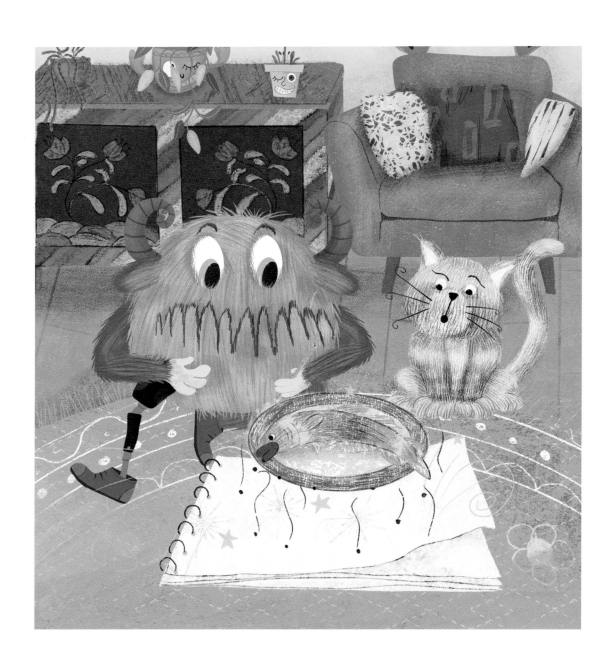

Kit got a cod.

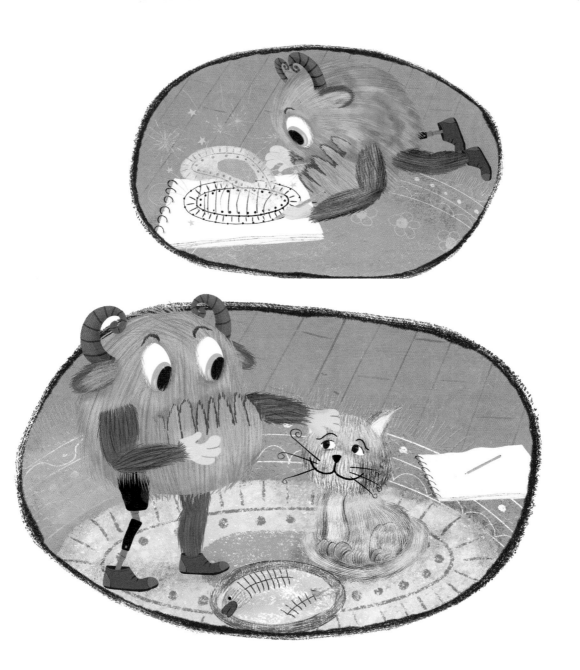

Kit got a mat and a pat.

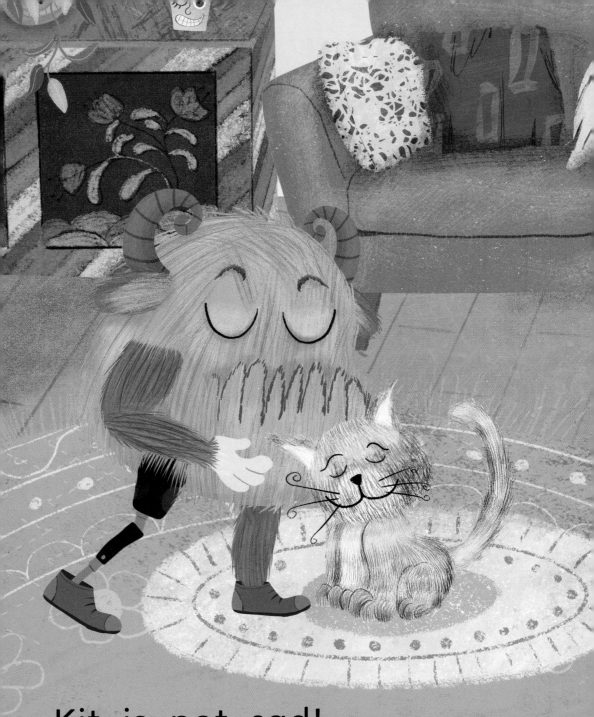

Kit is not sad!